♂ THE ♀ SEX MANUAL FOR PURITANS

VERNARD ELLER

WITH A FOREWORD BY RICHARD ARMOUR

Nashville ABINGDON PRESS New York

THE SEX MANUAL FOR PURITANS

Copyright © 1971 by Abingdon Press

All rights in this book are reserved.
No part of the book may be reproduced in any manner whatsoever without written permission of the publishers except brief quotations embodied in critical articles or reviews. For information address Abingdon Press, Nashville, Tennessee.

ISBN-0-687-38309-9
Library of Congress Catalog Number: 78-160793

SET UP, PRINTED, AND BOUND BY THE PARTHENON PRESS, AT NASHVILLE, TENNESSEE, UNITED STATES OF AMERICA

CONTENTS

(1) FOREWORD *by*
Dr. Richard Armour 11

(2) FOREWARNED *by*
the Rev. (Revolutionist) Cotton Picken **Mather** 13

(3) FORWORSE *by*
Dr. Vernard Eller 24

Chapter 1
EVERYTHING YOU ALWAYS ASSUMED
YOU KNEW ABOUT SEX 27

Chaper 2
SEX FOR FUN AND PROFIT 37

Chapter 3
WHAT TO LOOK FOR IN A PARTNER...45

Chapter 4
FOREPLAY 53

Chapter 5
POSITIONS 62

Chapter 6
THE CLIMAX 69

Chapter 7
AFTERWORD by the Rev. Mr. Mather 74

Preface
LONG AFTERWARD by Dr. Eller 76

IF APRIL SHOWERS BRING MAY FLOWERS,
WHAT DO MAY FLOWERS BRING?

For the answer, turn the page (which would be the logical thing to do now in any case).

MAYFLOWERS BRING THE REV. [Revolutionist] COTTON PICKEN MATHER AND HIS PURITAN SEX REVOLUTION

(1) FOREWORD
by
Dr. Richard Armour
author of A SHORT HISTORY OF SEX *and many other funny books*

Dr. Vernard Eller is no sex maniac. He is not even very sexy, although this is something you can never be sure about. He is probably just about normal, whatever that is. From the books you read about sex, being normal isn't normal these days. And being abnormal isn't as abnormal as it once was.

Being normal may, in fact, be the most unusual thing about Dr. Eller. He isn't a square, and he isn't a round —or a rounder. Perhaps you could say he is a square with rounded corners. In addition to the five physical senses, he has two senses that are rare in a writer about sex: common sense and a sense of humor.

These take him a long way and in an unusual direction. They keep him from getting too far out—or too far in. They keep him from writing about sex in a slimy,

11

prurient way. Instead of being sensual, he is sensible. If he isn't sexy, he is sensy.

Dr. Eller is also helped by being happily married and by being a popular teacher. Happy married life is usually indicative, among other things, of a happy sex life—at home. Being a popular teacher, especially with today's college students, usually indicates knowledge of one's field and, above all, the ability to communicate this knowlede to others, even when they don't want it.

Because he is an unusual person, Dr. Eller has written an unusual book about sex. It is a book that keeps within the bounds of good taste, though being frank and forthright. It is practical, positive—and decent. One thing it is not is dull.

In these pages Dr. Eller proves that sex is both fun and funny. Or perhaps that people are funny about sex. Since people are funny about everything, this isn't too hard to prove.

—R.A.

(2)
FOREWARNED
by the Rev. Cotton P. Mather

It may be a mad thought, but it needed to be thunk. When those who can think won't, some of the rest of us must stand ready to take over.

IF EVERYONE ELSE HAS SEX BOOKS THESE DAYS, WHY SHOULDN'T PURITANS HAVE THE RIGHT TO OWN AND READ THEM TOO?

There is in our fair country (some would call it "great," but in light of the situation here to be exposed it must be rated only "fair") a suppressed, enslaved, and dehumanized minority from which we have not heard.

You may find that hard to believe, because the general impression is that the pie has been so divided that anybody could identify with one downtrodden minority or another. But here is a group that has been so completely suppressed that it hasn't even been granted the right to consider itself a suppressed minority. And that just isn't fair. I mean, if some people get the fame and attention of being a suppressed minority, it isn't fair to deny the privilege to others simply because they aren't smart enough to realize how suppressed they really are. So I hereby am volunteering to step into the breach and assume the humanitarian obligation of helping these poor people achieve their rightful dignity and status as social outcasts.

We live in a day in which presumably every person can own and enjoy sex literature. The newsstands abound with it. The bestseller lists aren't long enough to credit the worthy entrants. All respectable homes (and many unrespectable ones) have the material gracing coffee table and nightstand, readily accessible for the edification of the entire family. Because of the modern miracle of this literary campaign, no child need grow up in the dark about sex (very little of it any longer taking place in the dark). He may not learn what the game is all about, but he certainly will be familiar with the layout of the playing field.

It must be said, too, that by far the greater part of this literature is very well done indeed. It goes into the subject thoroughly, not neglecting any detail that might improve or titillate the reader. And the usefulness of much of the material is enhanced by the fact that it is laviciously illustrated with authentic pornographs of prominent modules in appalling poses, risqué in detail and with every nuance exquisitely limned. Viewing these beauties is an education in itself; here, perhaps

Forewarned

for the first time, a young person can see people as they really are—women who are really (and obviously) women and men who appreciate the fact.

And yet, although it is difficult to believe that this could happen in a society that calls itself civilized, there is in our midst a sizable number of those who are deprived of this literature solely on the basis of a religious-philosophical prejudice, namely that they wouldn't be caught dead with it. These are the Puritans—good, upright (don't you dare change that "r" to a "t"!) citizens in their own way—and yet discriminated against for no reason other than the color of their blue noses.

Thoroughly aroused over this shocking state of affairs, I determined that there should be at least one sex book that Puritans *could* be caught dead with, one lavishly illustrated and exquisitely limned book that they might find in *their* bookstores and have on *their* coffee tables.

AND THIS FAIR VOLUME (sorry, "great" volume) IS IT!

In preparing to commission the writing of the book, it soon became apparent that there is only one man who could do the job (better—only one man who even would consider doing the job). Eller; who else?

Vernard Eller is eminently qualified. In the first place, he is as puritanical as they come. I mean, anybody that would write a book taking the position that MAD magazine preaches the Ten Commandments must be a moral cultist of one sort or another. And as you may recall, his *MAD Morality* ($2.79 cheap) was nothing if not prim and prudish.

The Sex Manual for Puritans

In the second place, he is a doctor; and any sex book worthy of the name must be written by a doctor.

"But," it may be protested, "Eller is a doctor of *theology*. He's not an M.D.—much less a psychiatrist."

That quibble, I am sorry to say, displays nothing but anti-Puritan prejudice. It is so easy for non-Puritans, thoughtlessly and without considering other points of view, simply to assume that sex is nothing more or less than bodily function. However, the Puritans maintain that, if man is created in the image of God and destined for his kingdom, sexual questions (and answers) are at base as much theological as they are medical, physiological, or psychological. At least this is what Dr. Eller undertakes to prove. And it would seem to be only fair that a doctor of Eller's variety be given opportunity to challenge these M.D.'s at their own game and produce a *theological* sex manual.

"But what could a clod like Eller know about *sex*?" I hear the skeptics sneering.

Well, it is true that the good doctor must admit that the totality of his experience has been with one woman (who is now—and always has been—Mrs. Eller, he insists that we add).

But this fact indicates more than is immediately apparent. I suppose everyone has heard the story about the little moron who kept sawing back and forth on just one string of his violin, playing the same note over and over while the other children in music class were ranging all over the scale. "Why are you fiddling around *that* way?" the teacher asked. "Why not?" the little

Forewarned

moron replied. "The rest of the kids are still looking for the right note, but I've found it."

Everyone knows that story, but what is not generally known is that the name of the little moron was Eller. But it makes sense. The guy who is out to take sex wherever he can get it is hardly the expert; he's fumbling and groping for what he is not expert enough to find. But the man who can hit it right the first time and so never feel the need to go elsewhere—that man is the authority on sex. And on that count Dr. Eller is an authority. Besides, he was locker-room attendant for the football team when he was in junior high school, and those fellows taught him all about sex. They even taught him some things that haven't been discovered yet. What Dr. Eller can't tell us about sex would better be left untold.

But what he has written must be read against the background of the intolerable sex setup into which a pig society has forced its Puritan minority. All in the world the Puritan asks is the right to live his own life in his own way. But what chance has he got when the whole deck is stacked against him, deliberately arranged to cream him off?

Go to the movies (or as many as they will let you into); what is there that an honest Puritan could relate to? Watch the teevies—including the commercials that are selling every product under the sun and yet all selling sex in the process. What place does a Puritan have in that mix? Flip through the magazines, scan the paperback titles, walk through a bookstore. Can you understand why a Puritan feels that there is nothing there that expresses *his* longings and aspirations, that is food for *his* soul? Look at the record jackets; listen to the lyrics and the beat—the orgiastic frenzy of the beat. Ours is a world that affords no place for the Puritan, that is intent to make him an alien in his own homeland.

Black culture has won a place in society. There are many black books on the market today—black history, black poetry, black drama, black art. There are black fashions, black music, black food, black politics, and black theology. But where can the despised Puritan find room for his life-style?

Clearly, his enemies are in the saddle and are intent to trample down every vestige of his once proud culture. Impious imperialistic Impuritanism controls the establishment and is practicing genocide—yes, planned and deliberate genocide—against a defenseless and innocent people whose only crime is that they stand for purity, truth, and godliness.

Imagine, if you can, the inhuman situation that I have witnessed with my own eyes: a fine, once-respected Puritan mother and father standing by helplessly as they view their own children being slowly but inevitably sucked into the maelstrom of rampant Impuritanism, able to do nothing as they see them gradually degenerate to the point that some even subscribe to *Playboy*. It is not a pretty thing to watch, I can assure you; and yet this is happening thousands of times a day in the streets of our cities and even in our own homes. Each and every Puritan is fair game for the machinations of these foul hedonists; and unless they are stopped soon,

Forewarned

the glories that once spelled Puritanism may be forever extinguished from the face of the earth.

As the Streete-Korner Report has made so very clear, the evil that underlies the entire situation is Impuritanism—nothing but Impuritanism. However, this is not to say that the mass of people by this token are consciously and deliberately Impuritanist; they don't have to be. Impuritanism is built into the very foundations of our society and infects every aspect of its procedures and structures. We don't have to be Impuritan; our social organization is such as to destroy the Puritans without our personally lifting so much as a finger against them.

Perhaps the most malicious aspect of the whole sordid affair has to do with the sexual myths that are perpetrated against these innocent people. These become the excuse for any crime against them and are read back into the very roots of the Puritan tradition; from that point they become accepted as self-evident and long-established truth.

For instance, most people believe that in their natural state Puritans display no sexual markings. This is a vicious slander. Just because the New England fathers (and mothers) chose not to heed the modern injunction to "let it all hang out" does not mean that down underneath they were not differentiated into the same categories that are so readily apparent today. Now it may be true that clothes make the man, but it also is true that clothes do not prevent one from being a woman. Reputable scholars have established conclusively that Puritan babies were born in the same state of undress as other babies and that, analyzed under such conditions,

The Sex Manual for Puritans

the same distinctive configurations could be observed as in their modern counterparts. It is safe to assume, too, that these distinctions persisted into adulthood and probably even became intensified through the years.

Also, there is good evidence that the Puritans always have known how to put these distinctions to use. The very fact that Puritan babies were born—and born naked —surely is to be taken as an indication that they were conceived in the same way (i.e., conceived through the same sort of activity that is known to produce naked babies today).

And the fact that Puritan women tended to have *many* babies would suggest that, far from being sex*less,* they were most sucsex*full* in promoting what in ecumenical circles is known as "organic union."

Further, the fact that their success was, in almost every case, monogamous, repeated, frequent, and of long duration may be taken as evidence that the Puritans had learned not only how to use sex but also how to enjoy it. Surely the transiency and profligacy of contemporary sex is a poor basis for the boast against Puritans that moderns are doing it more because they are enjoying it more. With sex as with smoking, the truth is probably quite the reverse.

This brings us to the finding that should put the Impuritans in their place and squelch their calumnious myth-making for all time. It is what has come to be known as the Probity Principle. We hinted at it a bit earlier:

In the symphony of sex, that moron is the maestro who begins on the right note and stays with it rather

Forewarned

than fiddling around all over the place. By this measure, the modern disciples of Impuritanism certainly are in no position to belittle the sex life of the despised blue-noses.

Indeed, we now have exposed the fallacy that underlies the entire Impuritan argument. The assumption is made that, because Puritans have chosen not to all the time be talking about sex and flaunting it in the faces of everyone around, this must be a sign that they are afraid of it, unhappy over it, uncomfortable with it. And on the contrary, the modern, easy familiarity with sex is taken as a sign that it has been tamed, that everything is under control, and that joy reigns supreme.

Pornographic postulations! The assumption is manifestly muddled and flagrantly false! I have one friend who, in all our long association, has never once brought up or shown any particular inclination to discuss the subject of TIGERS. But I have another friend who is always talking about tigers—what fine animals they are; how, next to dogs, they are man's best friend; what fun it would be to frolic with them; etc.; etc.

Now I happen to know that my first friend's silence is occasioned by the fact that his association with tigers is everything it should be; he is on good terms with every tiger he knows; he feels secure and content in all his tiger relationships. But my second friend's interminable tiger talk is what is known as "whistling in the dark." Actually, he is afraid that the tigers are about to get loose and come eat him up. His big talk is an effort to convince himself that he likes tigers and that they like him (in the non-gastronomical sense of the

The Sex Manual for Puritans

term), that there is no threat. In reality his obsession must be seen as a symptom of insecurity and fear that the situation might be more than he can handle.

Just so, any sexually secure Puritan knows that the show and tell of today's Impuritan obsession is motivated by a fear that sex is getting loose, that its significance and value are threatening to dissolve, that it bids fair to chew up the keepers who feed it.

It should be obvious, then, that the present sexual establishment is not only criminally repressive toward guileless Puritans but is itself inwardly corrupt, supported only by flimsily fabricated myth.

So where's the revolution that is truly revolting? Well, it certainly does not lie with Con III and the Greedy-Groined Grieving of America. (For those who are not yet in the know, Con I, II, and III are shorthand symbols. Concupiscence I designates *geneal lust*, the desire to build home and family and further the *generation* of the race; Concupiscence II designates *genitive lust*, the desire to acquire *possession* and savor wealth, status, and mastery; and Concupiscence III designates *genital lust*, the desire to attain high heat and enjoy a large charge.)

It is, then, this Con III establishment that must be brought down; it has no right to exist. We will be justified in using whatever means are necessary. If we must, we can rape, lewd, and burn (although it may be better to marry, as the Apostle Paul suggests); but Puritanism *will* come into its own.

So the word is:

Off the Impuritans! Make them grovel in their filthy

Forewarned

orgies (which is what they are inclined to do anyhow)! Arise all ye Puritans of purely pure purity! Bring in the day of true brother-and-sisterhood, and end the night after night of wrong!

ALL POWER TO THE PEEPERS (i.e., to those who peep, not for their own enjoyment—heaven forbid! —but only to keep track of the nasty naughties of the Impuritans)!

The Revolution (the *Puritan* Revolution) is here! It's happening!

And every revolution worth its salt must have a manifesto and a manual. This here is the manifesto, and the pages that follow are the manual. So revolt away!

—C.P.M.

(3)
For Better
or
FORWORSE
by
Dr. Vernard Eller

(If we can maintain this foreword motion long enough, the writing of the book itself will be for better.)

I have some difficulty digging Mather's blather; I can't figure out what he has in mind when he goes so completely ape over the Puritans. For one thing, the difficulty of such figuring is aggravated by the fact that the *amount* of mind involved is strictly minimal. Also, it might be noted that, for some people, "going ape" entails a much shorter trip than it does for others.

My guess is that he is playing up to the Puritans in hopes of selling books to them. But this strikes me as being a most futile strategy; there just aren't that many Puritans around any more. And even if there were, no one in his right mind would be fool enough to let himself be identified as such. In our day, to be called a Puritan is the ultimate put-down, seeing as how Puri-

Forworse

tanism is considered the ultimate hang-up. As everyone knows, all that prevents today's Con III folk from breaking free and bringing in the Golden Age are the repressions and timidities inherited from the Puritans.

Nonetheless, even if it means that we do not sell a single copy, I am willing to stand with Mather as the last of the Puritans and write his book for him—if *I* get to say what Puritanism means. *His* ravings on the subject could get the book censored and ourselves shot.

My interest is not in trying to rescue the reputation of the New England forefathers—although my suspicion is that they have been done a grave injustice. The facts, I believe, would not support the assertion that it is they who are preventing the birth of a new humanity. Even as regards sex, it cannot be demonstrated that they branded it as altogether sinful and shameful, as something to be as little enjoyed and as much suppressed as possible. It cannot even be sustained that their sexual conversation and deportment were as prissy and uptight as current caricature would have it.

But my purpose in this book is not to argue what those Puritans may or may not have been. The history likely does need straightening out, but I am not the man to do it.

Currently, however, it tends to be taken as axiomatic that to restrain sex in any way is to hamper its value and limit its enjoyment. "Puritanism," then, is used as the label for any thought or activity that advocates the discipline or control of sex as over against its completely free and untrammeled expression.

But if this is what is meant by Puritanism, then I

The Sex Manual for Puritans

am altogether ready and willing to be called a Puritan. My deep conviction and the thesis of this book is that, *with the proper sort of controls properly applied,* both the value and fun of sex are enhanced rather than curtailed.

You decide whether or not that puts me into a class with this Mather character and his kind. If so, then the whole point of our book can be stated even more simply:

>PURITANS HAVE MORE SEX FUN THAN ANYBODY!

Chapter One
(or Four, depending upon how you count Forewords)

EVERYTHING YOU ALWAYS ASSUMED YOU KNEW ABOUT SEX*

*And So Didn't Bother to Ask

It is true that this chapter heading bears a certain superficial resemblance to the title of the popular book by Dr. David Reuben (M.D., as you might guess). That could be sheer coincidence.

Well, it *could* be!

Yes, he did write his book first, but you can't prove that I didn't *think* of mine first. Actually, there are two main differences between his book and mine. In the first place, his doesn't have any pictures, and mine has some lulus ("every nuance exquisitely limned"). In the second place, his book is one of the all-time bestsellers; as of this writing, mine hasn't sold a copy.

Everything You Always Assumed

Nevertheless, Reuben's book needs mine (he hasn't admitted that, but I will). His tells only half the story of sex—although the half that sells books, it must be noted. The half he does tell, he tells thoroughly and well. All the ins and outs of sex as bodily activity (of infinite variation) get described in detail. But Reuben pictures man too small. Oh, it is true that he points out that the largest and most important of man's sex organs is his brain; but he does not sufficiently recognize that, through his brain, man's sex gets linked up with a great many other interests and functions as well. Reuben fails to treat the sex beyond sex, as it were.

Our two books, then, can divide the field between them. I do not propose to handle the aspects of sex which he treats. Likewise, he hardly touches upon what I propose to treat. The difference, however, is this: I am well aware (sometimes too much aware) of sex as bodies in motion and glands in commotion. I am happy to grant the validity and need for his book and the sort of sex education it represents. However, I am not sure that he shows a similar awareness of the story I want to tell.

The point I am intent to make should be obvious enough. It is, therefore, the Eller Elucidation: **A person is bigger** (or should be bigger) **than his sex organs** —even if his brain is counted among his sex organs.

The view of man underlying Reuben's book is deficient. Whether or not it marks his deliberate position, he manages to leave the impression that human beings essentially are discrete atoms, each propelled by his "pulsating genitals" (Reuben's phrase) whose thrust should not and ultimately cannot be denied. His concern, then, is that, as these atoms bump into sexual contact one with another, the vibrations between them be as good as possible. He is emphatic that the secret lies much more in the state of the brain than in the form and comeliness of the other apparati involved. He shares countless helpful hints on how to insure high-level vibes. He makes a strong case for the fact that homosexuality and relations with prostitutes almost inevitably fail to produce quality experience.

All this is well and good, but it needs to be recognized that a human being is much more than just a giant spermatozoon jetting around at random until it happens to find its destiny in a happy bump and boinn-ng. If men are atoms, they are the sort that are unstable until they have joined with other atoms in the formation of a molecule—molecule then joining with molecule in the formation of a compound; particle then joining with particle in the formation of an object; object then joining with object in the formation of a universe. (Whoever thought up the idea of calling the conglomeration in which we live a *"uni*verse" did well; certainly the intention behind it is that everything be integrated into a well-ordered whole, even though we may be a long way from achieving such coordination in fact.)

But this sort of "build in here," "tie together there," "weld another piece on that point," "consolidate this structure into that larger pattern"—this sort of construction is something far different from bump/vibrate/"yecch!"; bump/vibrate/"interesting!"; bump/vibrate/

Everything You Always Assumed

"fair!"; bump / vibrate / "heaven!"; bump / vibrate / "I should a stood in heaven!"

Our view of man sees his life as consisting in *commitments* rather than mere *experiences*. A man and a woman commit themselves to each other to form a marriage. The commitment is enlarged and new commitments are made to form a family. Both individuals and families make additional commitments to form communities of many different sorts. Communities make mutual commitments to form peoples and nations. Peoples and nations *should* commit themselves to one another to form the family of man. And the family of man *should* commit itself to live in harmony with the world of nature.

And according to the view here being developed, this overall commitment-structure is not thought of as the spontaneous invention of men, a parlor game in which each successive generation adds a paragraph to an undirected and entirely open-ended story. Rather, all these human commitments are to be seen within the commitment of the Author and the story he is intent to tell. His is the story of the creation of a *uni*verse (actually the re-creation of a universe that had fallen apart when men decided that they would rather live by experiences than by commitments). By the way, the theological name for *uni*verse is "the kingdom of God," because the only commitment that ultimately carries any hope of integrating the present *"untidy*verse" is commitment to the kingly rule of God.

It is this consideration that gives sex its theological dimension. On first thought it might seem as though this view of life—which is as broad as the universe itself and as long as the stretch from its first creation to its final re-creation—reduces the significance of an individual man and his actions to almost nothing. Quite the contrary, here is the setting which for once recognizes the true importance of the individual. The universe is built through, is constructed out of, human commitments; and human commitments, whether made alone or in concert with others, cannot be made other than by individual humans. Without *your* help the consummation of the universe is hindered in its coming.

Puritanism, then (our brand of Puritanism), does not disparage the individual or even what Reuben refers to as the power of his pulsating genitals. To the extent that man is a sexual being (which is a considerable extent indeed), to that extent sex is one of the motivating powers behind his commitments, a power that has its part to play in the building of the universe.

Sex, then, is more important than Reuben would have it, not less so—and that precisely because sex is not an end in itself. In other words, flights of ecstasy do not mark the highest reward sex has to offer. Man's greatest satisfaction, joy, fulfillment, and usefulness come, not in romping around this world's playground for a few short years, but through making the commitments that build him into his proper slot in the universe that is coming to be. And not only does the individual find his own highest happiness by getting himself rightly positioned, he helps make the whole universe a happier place at the same time.

So, when a person is faced with the choice between

experiencing some better-than-ever sex vibrations or making (or standing by) a commitment that fits another piece into our erector-set universe, he would do well to sacrifice the first and go with the second. The power of sex can be dedicated to some great and lasting accomplishments.

Of course, if Dr. Reuben or anyone else can give some help that will upgrade the vibrations occurring within a universe-building commitment that already has been made, God bless him. And for that matter, the time-honored experience of high-class Puritanism has been that, in nine cases out of ten if not ninety-nine out of a hundred, one is more likely to achieve the heights of sexual ecstasy by working to improve the experience within his commitment, rather than by cutting out to chase a vision of sexual heaven through the bump/vibrate/bump/vibrate/bump method.

Profound *commitment to* another person is not at all the same thing as an overwhelming physical and emotional *experience with* another person. Yet these two tend to get all confused with each other, precisely because both are marked by deep personal involvement. (I am deliberately avoiding the word "love," because we are accustomed to use it to cover either or both elements indiscriminately.)

The difference is that commitment centers on duration, stick-to-itiveness, and lasting power, whereas experience has its end and goal in the moment of the experience itself. Thus, the young woman who defended her sex adventures on the grounds that they were motivated by *love,* that she gave herself completely and totally to each man she slept with, may have been telling as much of the truth as she understood, but it cannot have been the whole truth. She could mean only that she gave everything she could *to the experience that was taking place.* But obviously she did not understand this to entail giving herself *from this time forward,* giving every aspect of her life and her self (present and future) to be united with him.

Although there is much temptation to do so, the strength of one's commitment cannot be gauged by the excitement of the experiential moment but must be measured by the fidelity demonstrated in the absence of pleasurable experience and even in the face of negative experience. In the ecstatic instant of bump and boinn-ng anyone would like to have the experience go on forever and can fool himself into thinking that this feeling is the equivalent of an until-death-do-us-part commitment. Yet once the experience is over (and the very nature of the case dictates that there must be this sort of parting long before death effects it), the supposed commitment often proves as transient as the experience itself.

Now, of course, the best sort of sex is that which brings together long-term commitment *and* thrilling experience into one package. But even there the situation is not simply half of one and half of the other. The subtraction of one or the other does not leave equal remainders. Commitment is the much more crucial ingredient of the two.

Sexual *commitment* lacking the component of bodily sexual *experience* is *handicapped* sex, but handicaps can be overcome or risen above. The relationship still can be made a satisfying and significant one. For example, if a man became injured so that it were physically impossible for him to perform the sex act, it still would be quite possible for him and his wife to make adjustments permitting their marriage to continue as a very valid sexual relationship, i.e., a relationship made possible by and deriving its value from the fact that the partners are of opposite sexes.

But sexual *experience* lacking the component of *commitment* is *truncated* sex. A vital part is missing, and the couple has substituted a pathetic half-sex for what the relationship could be and was meant to be.

However, when Reuben fosters such implications as the suggestion that religious celibates (priests, monks, nuns, and others) necessarily are limiting their own humanity and depriving themselves of their true destiny as human beings, he is way off the mark. He does not acknowledge the possibility that these people may be using their sex power in a different way than most of us do—yet, even so, in a way that truly signifies sex dedicated to the highest goals of their own humanity and the humanity of the race.

You see, sex is one of the powers that propel men, but it is by no means the only one. Man's sex urges are part of a mix with a whole host of other urges and motivations—physiological, psychological, emotional, intellectual, and spiritual. The intention, then, is that the mix be governed by motives of the mind and will so that the whole moves the man in one direction (rather than a confusion of directions) and that the movement be along the vector that spells universe-building and true humanity. Puritanism asks, not that sex be denied, but that it be harnessed and put to work for both the individual's truest enjoyment and the achievement of his own humanity along with that of the rest of the world. Reuben's view of sex is seen to be not so much false as narrow.

The difference, then, between Puritanism and Impuritanism is not that Puritanism is opposed to sex while Impuritanism favors it. Not at all. Rather, Impuritanism values sex only for the experience, the good vibrations it provides. Puritanism enjoys good vibrations but sees that sex, when harnessed to commitment, also can be used to forward the greatest dreams of man and God.

So our battle cry is not "Down with Reuben; Up with Puritanism." It is:

"Come on Reuben, Rachel, and All the Rest. Think Big. Dream Sex Dreams that Can Take in the Whole of Humanity and a Real, True Universe. Join the Revolution!"

Chapter Two
SEX FOR FUN AND PROFIT

SEX IS FUN.

Actually it would be much closer to the truth to say that sex *can* be fun, for we would do well to keep in mind that, although sex is the source of some of the greatest pleasure people can know, it is also the source of some of mankind's greatest unhappiness, tragedy, and heartbreak. One dare not assume that whenever he has the opportunity to bump and boin-n-ng it automatically will turn out to be fun.

Nevertheless, sex can be fun. The Impuritan establishment, of course, is founded directly on this premise, and there is no need for us to write their propaganda for them. So you choose how the point best can be made. Space is left on this page for you to clip and paste

The Sex Manual for Puritans

in the testimony of your choice from whatever book, magazine, or newspaper you prefer. It may even be easier for you to find a picture that will make the point more graphically than any paragraph could. But we have no intention of arguing the matter: paste in what you will, and we will be quick to grant the point.

[Paste Here]

However, where Puritanism steals a march on Impuritanism is in showing that sex can pay a profit even while it is being fun.

Now don't jump to a conclusion and assume that we are talking about prostitution; it does not meet the test at all. True, it does bring an income—although it does not represent as clear and easy a profit as one might think. But more to the point, Dr. Reuben indicates that prostitutes derive very little fun from their activity. Or if it is fun, it is fun of a most perverted sort. He

Sex for Fun and Profit

says that prostitutes are motivated primarily by a *hatred* of men, and their satisfaction comes from taking the poor John's money and giving nothing—absolutely nothing of themselves in return. So not only does the prostitute derive no true pleasure from her sex, but the profit itself is nothing but stolen goods.

But if we could find a way in which sex would retain its fun and yet pay a good, honest income—that would be a real deal, because the pleasure of fun increases geometrically as one is paid for doing it. For instance, putting out 50¢ to ride on the merry-go-round is one thing; getting a free ride is something else; but to be paid good wages for simply riding a merry-go-round?— man, nobody ever yet has rated a setup like that!

Maybe not; yet this is precisely what Puritanism has to offer—and regarding sex even, not just bloodless and cold merry-go-rounds!

There is only one condition for reaping the double payoff of both fun and profit: the sex has to take place within that commitment called *marriage*.

We must be very clear at this point about what "marriage" is precisely. Although virtually all true marriages will be licensed by the state (and rightly should be), this is not to say that licensing is what makes a relationship a marriage. There are very many licensed liaisons which are not marriages by a long stretch, and in rare instances there may be true marriages which never have been licensed.

We need to give a moment's thought to this last point. Within the Impuritan establishment there is these days a great deal of wondering why it shouldn't be possible

—because marriage is not dependent upon a license—to have our marriages without all the bother and rigamarole of licensing. A marriage would be the truer and more beautiful, they say, if it were not propped up by legal involvements and guarantees; one could then be free to love in the name of love alone.

There is usually a considerable amount of hokum—deliberate or otherwise—involved here. Just follow up these licenseless relationships, and my guess is that it soon would become apparent that in very few if any instances was it the case that the marriage commitment went so deep that the idea of licensing was an insult. Rather, the commitment was quite shallow—so shallow, indeed, that there was an instinctive fear that legal safeguards might impede its easy dissolution.

But consider what was said in the previous chapter about marriage being a commitment that normally and naturally leads to wider commitments involving children, family, community, and society at large. This means that marriage, although highly *personal,* is not a purely *private* affair. Society has a real stake in it and thus is entitled to know who is married to whom, who is responsible for supporting whom, who is obligated to take care of what babies may come. This sort of announced intention is what licensing represents; and there would seem to be very few valid reasons why a couple that desires true marriage should want to evade this responsibility to their fellowmen.

However, the point we wanted to make is that being married and being licensed are not at all the same thing. "Marriage" is that quality of mutual commitment in

Sex for Fun and Profit

which a man and a woman determine that their respective slots in the plan of the universe are in fact one slot, that the humanity of each is to be found in relation to the other, that each is to seek the good of the other as being his own good, that they are going to stand or fall together—for richer or for poorer, in sickness or in health, until death do them part.

Given this sort of setting, sex takes on all sorts of great dimensions that it cannot begin to sustain otherwise. For a starter, the intimacy created by this quality of commitment makes the sex action all the looser, freer, and more fun; there are no inhibitions arising out of suspicion that one partner may not be giving himself as wholeheartedly as the other. And, catch this, the fun of the sex has the effect of driving the mutual commitment all the deeper. This is the snowball effect, in which the fun doubles the profit while the profit is doubling the fun; we will encounter the phenomenon time and again.

And in this regard it seems to be much more often the case that poor marriage commitments produce bad sex vibrations than that poor sex knowledge and technique hurts marriages. So let Dr. (M.D.) Reuben work his angle on the ways and means of bodily delight; there still is room for Dr. (Th.D.) Eller to work his angle of men and women under God becoming so committed to each other that all the delights of body, mind, and spirit are enhanced.

But we need to become much more specific about the actual profits that can be realized from married sex fun.

The Sex Manual for Puritans

In the first place, there are babies—a priceless dividend. It may well be that we are moving into a time when the *number* of babies will need to be severely limited; but you better believe it, babies still are going to be wanted, valued, and loved. It is a true instinct that says that babies are nice things to have around and that they have a big role to play in mankind's progress toward a human universe.

A wanted baby, in a marriage, is a very valuable asset. Not only are babies fun, more often than not their coming is the most effective means possible for deepening a marriage relationship. It's the snowball effect again: sex fun produces baby; baby deepens marriage commitment; deepened commitment enhances sex fun.

A child born to unmarried parents (which, remember, includes those who have gone through all the motions of license and wedding but who are not truly married) generally is a liability. An unwanted baby, bringing with him unwanted responsibilities, obviously is a liability in the eyes of his parents. But further, it is not fair to the baby to bring him into any situation but a true marriage. Whatever lack of marriage there is between the parents is a detriment to the baby; and these days (as always) babies need everything going for them they can get.

But the profits do not stop with the production of babies; not at all. For the mother and father to be deriving deep satisfaction from their sexual activities is one of the best things that can happen to a child growing up in a home. The happiness of the parents,

Sex for Fun and Profit

the rightness of their commitment, their fun, rubs off on the child and has a great deal to do with determining whether he will be a healthy and happy person for the rest of his life. Indeed, the happy marriage and sex relations of the parents constitute the best thing that can be done to insure happy marriage and sex relations for the child in his turn. It's the old snowball again: good sex in a good marriage produces good sex and good marriages from generation unto generation; poor sex in non-marriages (the licensed as well as the unlicensed) tends to perpetuate itself likewise.

But we are not done yet; sex profit can be compounded to achieve fantastic increments. Sex that is used to make a husband and wife more committed to each other and to their family produces a well-being that rubs off not only on their children but on the world at large. Sex, rightly applied, can be a major force in moving our untidyverse toward a universe.

That may strike you as a rather extravagant claim and a glob of high-flown religious nonsense. It is not; it is a scientific conclusion based on sound empirical evidence. A British social anthropologist, J. D. Unwin, spent seven years making a very extensive and detailed historical study of eighty different cultures old and young. His findings were then confirmed by the further researches of Pitirim Sorokin. The conclusion is that "civilization and culture depend on the regulation of sexual expression and the confinement of sexual intercourse to monogamous homes, and that where people are sexually 'free' and permissive, their culture deteriorates."

Sex, when its power is channeled through *commitment,* works toward bringing people together, building them into the social patterns that make for a harmonious, smoothly operating whole. Sex, when it is turned loose simply to seek *experience,* dissolves society into a swarm of isolated atoms. It is clear that we presently live in a society where the tendency is toward fragmentation rather than coalescence. Nevertheless, there is in this society a youth subculture which professes great concern about building a world of brotherhood, justice, peace, and love. Even so, this same subculture includes the proposal of going the route of increased sexual permissiveness. But this is to try to ride off in two different directions at the same time; it won't work. Puritan goals cannot be achieved by Impuritan means.

Sex for fun *and* profit? You bet! And the best part of the deal is that the way to have maximum fun is to play it for maximum profit at the same time.

Chapter Three
WHAT TO LOOK FOR IN A PARTNER

Who makes it best? How do you choose?

The first and most important principle of sexual choice is that it be made through the conscious and deliberate faculties of the mind rather than letting those pulsating genitals call the shots. If, as Dr. Reuben says, the brain is the largest of man's sex organs, it seems only fair that it should have the biggest say as to when and how the sex organs are to be used. This choice is too important, has too much of either happiness or unhappiness riding on it, to turn the decision over to one's animal instincts. Human beings were given intellectual capacities above the other animals expressly that they might use them to advantage, to the enhancement of the fun and profit of the whole creation.

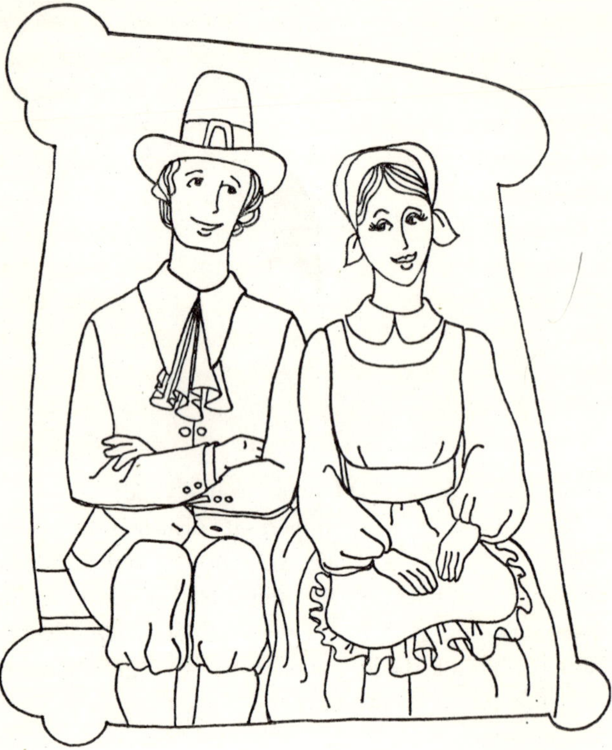

What to Look for in a Partner

After one has decided to use his head, the first thing he should understand with it is that there is no particular correlation between sex appeal (i.e., visual attractiveness either of the overall physique or of the sex organs themselves) and sexual performance. Dr. Reuben points out that almost every human being has all the physical apparatus required (or that can be used) for sexual enjoyment, and that normally no sort of examination or measurement of the equipment gives any clue to its effectiveness in use.

Certainly there is nothing wrong with choosing a beauty queen or a lifeguard (depending upon which sex is choosing which, of course), but, for goodness sake, don't make the choice simply because she is a beauty queen or he a lifeguard. Physique is irrelevant to the matter at hand.

Physique is not a positive sign of what to look for, but according to Reuben, an eagerness to show that physique is definitely a *negative* indication. People who manifest an urge to display their sexual parts, either undraped or only minimally draped, either for fun or for profit, Reuben calls "exhibitionists." And under this category he includes not only the dirty old men whom we consider sick but also the stripteasers, topless dancers, *Playboy* centerfolds, and beauty queens (Reuben names beauty queens; I am not enough of an authority to) whom we consider as the healthiest of female flesh. The problem, Reuben says, is that more exhibitionists than not get a sexual gratification out of exhibiting; and the fact that they get their kicks out of being *seen* means that they feel no great need for the kicks that come from actually *being* a sex partner. Those who make the biggest *pitch* turn out to be no *catch* at all.

But in seeking out a sex partner, avoid at all costs those who are most eager to become sex partners. That may sound strange, but it is true: overeagerness in becoming a sex partner indicates a poor prognosis that the person will make a *good* partner. Such people are infected with a highly communicable disease—which disease, interestingly enough, also can be and is being communicated via the mass media. It is called *copiosa copulatio casualis* or, in lay parlance, "promiscuity."

"But where's the danger?"

Well, an *addict* is a person who just has to have something even when he knows it is risky, unwise, and likely to be regretted. A drug addict is a person who has to have drugs no matter what, and a sex addict is a person who has to have sex on the same basis. "Slave" is the only term to describe such a person; as it was put by one of them who wound up in the hospital, his body covered with dermatitis caused by venereal disease, "I've been led around by my 'gotta haves' all my life."

Such a person is not free to act according to the best insights and reasoning of which his head is capable, because the center of control has passed over to his pulsating genitals (although it is most likely that the fault lies not in his genitals but in a psychological hang-up of one sort or another that moved the control center downward).

But again, this is not the voice of religious piety speaking; it is scientifically established fact. Out of more than a hundred unmarried college girls who sought psychi-

What to Look for in a Partner

atric help in a large state university system, 86 percent had had sexual relations with at least one person and 72 percent with more than one person. This against the university-wide average of something less than 22 percent of college females having had premarital relations. The psychiatrist making the study concluded: "Students who are psychiatric patients are likely to be promiscuous. Many of these patients—both male and female—can be described as alienated, and alienated students are especially promiscuous. While the alienated student seems to be leading a stimulating sex life he frequently complains that it is unsatisfying and meaningless."

The same sort of unhappy sex slavery comes to light through a different study. It is an established fact that suicide and attempted suicide are particularly critical problems on college campuses. The rate is extremely high among those who married quite young and have not been married long. Many of these undoubtedly are marriages that were premature because of pregnancy, sexual overeagerness, or other reasons. Marriages in which the bride was already pregnant at the time of the wedding have the poorest record of success of any marriage category.

Yet this correlation between suicide and premature marriage is not the only significant one. Ninety percent of adolescent suicide attempts are made by girls, and a number of different investigators have determined that guilt over their own sexual license is a major factor behind this statistic.

As, in regard to drug addiction, the source of the difficulty seems to lie more deeply in psychological factors than simply in the availability of the drugs, so it seems to be with sex addiction. Yet what can it be called except "addiction" that leads a person into actions which he cannot even stand to live with after he has performed them?

But what it all comes to is that the more easily accessible a person is as a sex partner, the less likely you would want him.

"But, Dr. Eller—sir—your topic was 'What to Look for in a Partner.' All you've done is tell us what to look for to avoid; what are we supposed to look for to *find*? Some of us are interested in *finding* sex, you know!"

I know, and I was getting to that. Everything must be done in due course—particularly when dealing with those who may be tempted to "do coarse."

Sex is like oil. One does not look for oil by looking for oil; very little ever would get found that way. One looks for oil by looking for the sort of geologic terrain that is likely (in due course) to bear oil. Oil is found by seeking the promising context and then approaching the oil itself from the perspective of that context.

Likewise, sexual ecstasy is nowhere near as likely to be found by concentrating one's search on the organic union that is supposed to spell ecstasy as by seeking out the kind of site which innumerable researchers have found to be the one dependable location for the discovery of strong and continuing reserves of ecstasy. That site is *marriage*.

(Oh, you already had it figured that that is where I was going to come out? Congratulations! It shows that you are a very perceptive reader.)

What to Look for in a Partner

Within marriage (keeping in mind that, by "marriage," we mean a quality of commitment rather than merely an arrangement of licensing), all the factors are right for sex at its best. On the contrary, outside of marriage, many elements come into play that drastically cut the chances of successful sex. And more, to settle for this risky, second-best sex as a sort of holding operation until marriage comes along—or as an experimental stage on the way to marriage—usually proves to be a bad move. Second-rate sex tends to corrode a person's commitment-controllers. Comes the time to make the big commitment that could spell sexual fulfillment, and the controllers often won't respond. Experimenters do not make good committers; it is too hard to kick the experimenting habit and go for broke. And yet sex becomes great only when one is able to do precisely this—go for broke and give out with everything: body, soul, mind, and strength, till death do us part.

So, what to look for in a partner?

One to marry more than to bump and vibrate. One to live with rather than merely sleep with. One whose children you would love rather than regret. One whom you would rather be poor with than rich without. One whom you would rather see happy than be happy yourself. One with whom you would forego pleasure rather than make feel guilty. One who would agree to postpone the action to the end of making it better later. One whom you would want as partner even if the sex experience did not turn out to be the biggest thrill in the world.

Choose this one; take time to set up the situation

The Sex Manual for Puritans

right (namely by getting married); if you need to (which you likely won't), use Reuben or some other doctor of his sort to learn a little technique; and, friend, you are as much as guaranteed the greatest sex fun (and profit) of which you are capable. Try it any other way and you void the guarantee. So, go Puritan, the only way to lie.

Chapter Fore
FOREPLAY

He who laughs last laughs best.

You bet! And all these years the Puritans have been laughed at because they have chosen not to talk sex, sex, sex, night and day, nothing but sex. Well, catch this! Half the sex words the big talkers use, they don't even know what they mean.

For instance, this "foreplay" they brag so much about; do you know what they have in mind? Ten— maybe fifteen—minutes of fooling around in bed before comes the bump and the boin-n-ng! Fun? Sure, it's fun; but do they think that is all the *play* sex is *fore*? Ha!

Sexual foreplay, for a Puritan, does begin in bed— when he is a baby in bed with his mother, as he is nursed, cuddled, and bounced. Play? Obviously; babies love it (and mothers don't mind it too much, either).

But play leading up to sexual relations? Right on; I kid you not! A baby's being played with at this time, in this way, is a very important factor in determining the sort of sex partner he will turn out to be in years to come. Indeed, the play he gets from his mother here will stand him in good stead for the play he is to give later in that ten minutes preceding the bump and the boin-n-ng.

Nevertheless, much more of sexual foreplay takes place outside of bed than takes place in (and I am not thinking of the back seats of cars, either). As parents play with the child in all sorts of ways and in all sorts of situations, as parents play with each other in sight of the child, as the child plays with his brothers and sisters—the whole playful mix—it all makes its contribution to heightening his experience of the sex act when the time comes, because the whole secret is in learning how to give out with play and to receive the play given out by the other (although neither of these should be confused with what we mean by being "played out").

This, by the way, is another reason why parents, would-be parents, or could-be parents (which should about cover the spectrum) have some obligation to confine their sex to marriage. Every baby has a right to this sort of foreplay, and parents have failed in a rather serious way when they bring a baby into the world under conditions that deny it to him.

However, sexual foreplay does take on new and interesting dimensions when it graduates to the level of heterosexual awareness and intrigue.

No! We are not yet ready for the bump and the boin-

Foreplay

n-ng; far from it. That's the trouble with people nowadays. All the time hurry, hurry, hurry! Rush through the foreplay in order to get to the real thing—as though that is all there is to sex! With these people it is not so much fore*play* as fore*work* (often no longer than a fore*word*—which, in case you were wondering, is why this book has three of them; it is an effort to slow things down a bit). Play, in order to be *play,* has to be done *for its own sake;* it ceases to be play if used only as a means for getting to something else.

The stage of sexual foreplay we now are discussing is the time for boys and girls to get to know one another as persons—as boy persons and girls persons—through a wide range of activities together, and yet without making a big deal about pairing off and getting serious (which, again, is to take the play out of foreplay). This stage is very important to the entire sex process. When it is omitted or foreshortened—as modern pressures tend to do—the result often is the slavery of sex addiction described earlier. Sex that is impelled by its "gotta haves" is sex that never learned the relaxed leisure of foreplay.

At the proper time comes the foreplay of dating. Girls and boys begin to pair off, learning how to play on a one-to-one basis. While they are at it, they would do well to learn a wide repertoire of games. When bump-and-boin-n-ng is the only game a couple knows, the play inevitably is going to get stretched mighty thin—particularly when one considers that here are being learned the play skills for a lifetime.

At this point, then, these couples (who ought to be freely coupling—in the Puritan sense of that term—un-

The Sex Manual for Puritans

coupling, and recoupling) would be wise to concentrate on other games and leave bump-and-boin-n-ng until later. It is time to be thinking about commitment but not time to be making one yet. Hurried commitments almost invariably are poor commitments. As the wise old Puritans used to say, "Look before you leap." And the fact of the matter is that the game of bump-and-boin-n-ng involves major amounts of leaping whether the participants intend or desire it that way or not.

Then comes engagement. The foreplay and the fun begin to intensify as the commitment starts to jell. Engagement is designed specifically so that the intimacy of the play and the depth of the commitment can feed upon each other and develop together. To skip this period or to shorten it to the place that it becomes more of a bombing raid than what any communiqué would term an "engagement" often stunts the commitment and stuns the intimacy.

But although its major purpose is the nurture of commitment, engagement has another very important aspect also. This is its escape clause. Of course, most couples could care less—because they are *certain* that they will never need to use it. Many if not most couples, of course, do not use it. However, many others do use it to very good effect; and many others more would be better off if they had used it. When it becomes apparent that the commitment is not developing into a true marriage, the escape clause enables the couple to disengage with as little hurt and damage as possible. To break the engagement after it has declared itself to be a marriage always increases the pain and difficulty.

Foreplay

Consider, then, that to introduce the intricate intimacies of intercourse tends also to close off escape hatches, making unpromising engagements that much harder to dissolve. Of course, the rising intensity of the foreplay is making restraint more and more difficult, but those couples who are man (and woman) enough to do it are wise to keep their options open and retain the control in their heads rather than passing it over to their pulsating genitals. The important thing is to build their commitment as strong and deep as human skill and power (and, I would say, God's help) can accomplish.

Now I know that there are hordes of potent plungers who are impatient to the point of rut and rape over all this guff about years and years and years of foreplay. They aren't interested in all that. They'll worry about commitment if and when they need it. They'll do what they feel like doing now and handle the consequences in do coarse. Not for them this baby talk about milk and then meat. They want—and they are gonna have—meat now.

Two comments these people might take time to ponder. The word "foreplay," which we have used to identify all this preliminary activity, is meant as an accurate label. To call it "play" is to suggest that it has value in and of itself. It does not need the payoff of the big twang to make it worthwhile; this play is that which is most appropriate, most profitable, *and most enjoyable* for persons at their particular stages of development.

The truth of this observation would be quite self-evident—except for the fact that modern social pressures and persuasions have managed to brainwash people into believing that sex consists entirely in intercourse, only of orgasm, and that therefore our salvation and fulfillment as sexual creatures lies in getting to it . . . the quicker the better. And it is precisely at this point that the Puritan Revolution is going to need to focus its overthrow.

Second, these people who are so sure that they can handle their sex life according to their own rules and always make it come up roses ought to look around themselves a bit. Sexual disappointment and unhappiness in all their manifestations constitute one of the major evils plaguing our already overburdened society. The victims range from studs and nymphomaniacs who waste their lives chasing the unattainable star of ultimate experience to impotent and frigid half-humans whose genitals refuse to pulsate at all.

Foreplay

My guess is that a major share of these disasters can be attributed to faulty foreplay—either because the person felt he was good enough that he could afford to cut corners or because he got cheated out of what he should have received at one stage or another. And there's the rub: because sex-sick parents simply have not the wherewithal to produce a healthy setting for the sexual foreplay of their children, and because a sex-sick society scoffs at the need for such, the disease is self-perpetuating and bound to become endemic. All joking aside, it just might be that a Puritan Revolution is more crucial for the survival of our civilization than any of the revolutions being heralded so boldly today.

Yes, of course I know that some people defy all the sexual laws of God, man, and nature and still apparently manage to come out on top. Also, some guys fall off the top of twenty-story buildings without killing their fool selves. But what makes you think you should be so lucky? It still is true as another old Puritan slogan says: "Better safe than sorry!"

"Well, it took us the better part of a chapter, but we have finally made it to marriage, *real* foreplay, and a binge of bump and boin-n-ng (ah, bliss!)."

Hold on just one minute. I'm writing this book, and I'm the one who gets to say when the chapter is over. I'll take care to let you know.

As long as you insist on referring to that ten-to-fifteen minutes in bed as "the *real* foreplay," you are still going to have problems. That isn't enough play to do the job. A man and wife ought to learn how to sneak in a little foreplay every now and then, while clothed as well as

The Sex Manual for Puritans

unclothed, at any old time and any old place, even in front of the kids and other people (it is particularly important that some of it be done in front of the kids, because that way they get some foreplay of their own out of it).

Now of course, most of this should be what we might call "camouflaged foreplay"—although some of it can be and probably ought to be overtly sexual. There is no need to tell observers that what is going on is *sexual* foreplay (it isn't necessary either, to tell your partner that that is what it is), even though this is the very truth of the matter. And obviously, because the kids are supposed to be participants as well as observers, the kind that goes on in their presence should be of the camouflaged variety.

But this sex play can take the form of nudges, prods, whacks, or tweaks; the form of hugs, kisses, nuzzles, or wrestling matches; the form of winks, smiles, gestures, or jerks; the form of compliments, presents, teasing, or jokes (it is most helpful for parents to have some private jokes that mystify the kids; it keeps them aware that they are witnessing a relationship that has more to it than they yet can dig). This foreplay should take any and every form the couple can devise; but it probably is more important for them to work at these techniques than at those of the bawdy bed—these are usable much more often and so provide that much more of sex for everyone around.

And, beloved, when you have built up a head of steam with this anywhere-anytime-everywhere-all-the-

Foreplay

time foreplay, then the ten-to-fifteen minute session can itself take off from a very high level. And the bump and the boin-n-ng? Ah, bliss!
End of Chapter
(Aren't you glad you let me do it my way?)

Chapter Five
POSITIONS

Hoo, boy! This is the chapter where most marriage manuals really let themselves go—because it lends itself to such interesting illustrations and photographs, I suppose. Also, the positions of the partners—their accumbency, acclivity, accessibility, acrobativity, actuation, acceleration, acumination, and accuracy—this is the easiest aspect of the sexual experience to vary, diversify, and experiment with.

So whenever sex goes sick, the thing to try is a new position. "I'm sorry, dear, but we've come to the last one in the book, a Spanish invention called *el posturo ludicrusioso,* plate 101 on page 934. I know you had to go to the chiropractor last time; this could be different. But we've just got to find *something* that makes it!"

Positions

It is interesting that books of this sort—although more so in the past than now—were called *"marriage manuals."* "Unmarriage manual" would be nearer the truth of the matter. For one thing, when the relationship between a man and wife has come to the place that items of sex technique are a primary concern, it usually is obvious that the factors which truly are important for marriage already are long gone. For another, the chances of saving a marriage by introducing innovative interminglings for instant idyllics is about the same as for saving suicides who jump from the Golden Gate Bridge by painting the bridge a different color.

And yet . . . and yet in suggesting that one's position *vis-à-vis* hisorher partner is *the* key to sexual fulfillment, the manuals are just exactly right—or would be if they weren't so just exactly wrong.

(*"Vis-à-vis"* is a French term meaning "face-to-face." However, we do not intend it to suggest any limits regarding the positions involved but use it in the broad sense of "in relation to." "Hisorher," on the other hand, is an Ellerian term designed to bring both sexes under one umbrella and keep this book bisexual, as it were—our modest contribution to women's lib.)

The manuals, which are mostly propaganda pieces for today's sex kick, are wrong in suggesting that *physical* posture is normally a critical factor in great and good sex. After all, millions upon millions of people managed to become competent copulators before sex manuals even were invented; and even today millions make it without the help of manuals. If these books were purchased only by people who actually need instruction

The Sex Manual for Puritans

in positional technique and whose relationship truly is improved through use of a book, my guess is that the publishers would go broke.

For the truth is that learning the mutual operations of anthropological sex equipage is not the same sort of problem as learning to drive an automobile. For one thing, it is a two-man rather than a one-man job (here using "man" in the sense that embraces woman). It employs (or should employ) only union labor. There is (or should be) much better communication between operator and equipment. The equipment is (or should be) much more responsive and cooperative than is the case with most automobiles. And above all, human beings have been made for each other in a way that cars and drivers simply were not; there have been provided instincts which can be counted upon to get the job done one way or another. And whether or not it has been well done is entirely for the participants to say;

Positions

the opinion of experts has nothing to do with the matter.

Thus, in all but the most exceptional cases, the manuals with their position papers are superfluous. On the other hand, they are positively harmful if they disturb contented people into thinking that some sort of sexual paradise lies just beyond them, attainable if only they can find the magic posture, grip, and swing (or, more often than not, the magic *partner*). But really, the surest way to spoil the fun of sex is to all the time be straining after something that most likely doesn't even exist. This is a transform play into work, fun into fear, and frolic into failure. It is the same sickness that plagues us elsewhere, but in this case it is known as "keeping up with the Johnson and Masters."

However, be that as it may, if "posture" is taken to signify, not the physical arrangement of the players, but how they are mentally, emotionally, and spiritually positioned toward each other, then posture is indeed the very pivot upon which sexual success turns.

Even so, when we make this change in the definition of "positions," we radically change the nature of the problem as well. Rearranging physical positions is easy, because the alignment of bodies is all that needs to be changed; the partners can go on being their normal, twisted, old selves. But finding new positions *vis-à-vis* each other as *persons* means that the partners themselves will need to be changed. ("Partners themselves being changed" is not at all the same thing as "a change of partners"—that last is a too-easy ploy which usually fails to accomplish anything except to shuffle the frustrated and compound their frustration.)

Moreover, when the question is that of physical correlation, there are any number of positions couples can assume and still be "right." If a position works, it is correct; and the manuals would indicate that the possibilities are amazing in scope and number. But when speaking of *human* correlation, there is only one position that is proper and that can be depended upon to work under all conditions, vine, verse, and adverse.

This one and only position is identified as "marriage." (Yes, we *are* going to go through all that again; after all, some readers may not catch on as fast as you do.)

Recall that marriage is not everything that the state has licensed or the church blessed as being such. It is precisely nothing more nor less than a particular position that a man and a woman can take *vis-à-vis* each other (and the stance is in every sense a *sexual* one, too). This relational posture is indeed a profound and subtle one, too fine and complex to be photographed as the other sex positions are—and thus not providing much in the way of exciting resources for illustrated manuals. Oh, certainly it is true that married people can be photographed; but photos of married people also can be posed, just as photos of other sex positions are. (Likewise, married people have been known to pose as unmarried.) But marriage itself is something that definitely cannot be posed. Posed marriages (of which our society is full) are actually no marriages at all.

Many details of the marriage posture can, of course, be varied at will; but the basic elements of the stance

Positions

are invariable. The fundamental feature is mutual commitment, his making her welfare his own and her making his hers. This commitment is connected to fidelity; fidelity is connected to trust; trust is connected to letting oneself go; and letting oneself go is connected to *getting* all of himorher; and it all is connected to de head bone. "Now hear de word of de Lawd!" (namely: "Therefore a man . . . cleaves to his wife, and they become one flesh" [Genesis 2:24]).

And hear this real good too: In spite of all manuals that imply otherwise, this authoritative Puritan manual is ready to proclaim that such a marriage posture is *the* position for sex.

That statement is correct but perhaps slightly misleading; it implies that the position is one thing and the sex something else that takes place out of and sequential to the position. But not so; the very *position* of marriage is a sexual relationship and would be so even if for some reason the act of physical intercourse could not take place. That is, it is a relationship based upon and made possible by the fact that he is a male and she is a female. The bump and boin-n-ng constitute simply one aspect (and not necessarily even the central aspect) of this larger and immensely grander sex act called "marriage."

It follows truly that intercourse apart from the context of marriage is a truncated and frustrated sex act. It may not be *coitus interruptus,* but it certainly can be described as *sexus interruptus*—and with many of the drawbacks of the former.

Buy all the manuals you can find, try all the positions

they suggest and invent some of your own; you won't find anything that even remotely approaches the thrill and bliss of the marriage posture. Conversely, once you get going on the marriage posture, you can throw the manuals away; in the great majority of instances questions of physical position naturally will answer themselves. Likewise, if you now are doing it more but enjoying it less (or doing it less because you aren't enjoying it anymore), you would be smart to try improving positions. But the one to work on is the marital rather than the coital.

Chapter Sex
THE CLIMAX

Do you know what most people have in mind when they talk about "sexual climax"? It is to laugh. The boin-n-ng. Yes, they're referring to the boin-n-ng. How about that?

How long does one last? Five seconds at most. And this they want to call the "climax" of sex. I figure a person must have a pretty small view of sex if he thinks it is something that can be climaxed in five seconds. For that matter, even if one were to add together the "climaxes" of a lifetime, it couldn't come to more than a few hours of big thrill. To live a lifetime as a sexual being for the sake of a scattering of spasmodic boin-n-ngs hardly seems a climax worthy of the name. This is not to deny that a boin-n-ng can feel real good, but *no* five-second trip is all *that* good.

The Sex Manual for Puritans

And yet, in very truth, all the puff and blow of today's sexual advertisement is designed to convince us that such climax is the be-all and end-all of sex, that it is indeed the be-all and end-all of life itself, the goal and crown that makes human existence worthwhile, the highest reach of the human spirit (well, not exactly "spirit," of course, but what passes for such in modern anthropology), and—as some theologians have implied—an equivalent of worship and sacrament. Being such, climactic highs are, of course, to be sought at all costs, doing whatever is necessary to collect them.

But Puritans know that this idea is a malicious lie aimed at cheating them out of the true climax of their sexual activity. They know what these "climaxes," these twangings of the glands, really amount to. By themselves they amount to diversions of the moment, giggles of gratification, the contemporary equivalent of bread and circuses. Nevertheless, when Puritan sex is set free and allowed full play in seeking its true climax, then these fleeting but fervid fragments become something else again, namely, signs, promises, and illuminational presentiments of that grand climax of which these are merely herald and servant.

"And what, pray tell, is this alleged GRAND CLIMAX? 'Marriage,' I suppose?"

Well, that isn't the very word I was going to use, but your guess shows that you are right in there with us.

Puritan thinkers argue among themselves as to just when and how the true sexual climax happens, but they have no problem as to where it lies. Some maintain that it comes with the birth of a baby—a loved, wanted,

The Climax

family-wrapped baby. Others would agree in principle but maintain that true sexual climax has been achieved only if the newborn infant is the couple's grandchild—demanding considerably less of floor-walking, nighttime feeding, and dirty diaper-changing than first-order babies do.

However, all are certain that the highest sort of climax centers in a house that sex built, a home where mother and father, grandpa and grandma, brother and sister, friends and playmates, and even the cats and dogs enjoy the good times (and the good people) that are produced, not simply by twanging glands, but by full-bodied, long-lasting, deeply rooted sex.

It is of course recognized that homes of this sort have a most ameliorative effect on the communities and society of which they are a part. Even so, there is some argument as to whether all of this joy, peace, and well-being can be claimed as *sexual* climax. More recently, however, there has arisen a radical school of Puritan theologians—derisively referred to as "the sex fiends"—who have dared to go even further. They claim that the ultimate sexual climax is what the Bible knows as "the kingdom of God."

Of course, very few garden-variety Puritans support this extremist view, but the logic of the "fiends'" position has proved hard to refute. Undeniably the kingdom of God marks the climax of the long-drawn contest between sin and righteousness which we know as "the human race." Undeniably, too, man (embracing woman) is a sexual creature. His sex is a vital part of

The Sex Manual for Puritans

his humanity and a motive power that can be of tremendous help in moving it toward its destiny.

Conversely, it is clear that fouled-up sex is one significant factor in the general foul-up of humanity under which we presently suffer. Thus, in the process of getting our overall humanity straightened out, God is going to *have* to straighten out man's sex life too. And if that achievement won't qualify as "sexual climax," I don't know what would; certainly no one would be so stupid as to choose any five-second eruption in place of *that!* The only smart alternative, then, is to set up the situation so that these short-burst experiences serve that one. Indeed, these deserve to be called "climaxes" only insofar as they mark progress toward a realized humanity, the end and goal for which sex was created in the first place.

Whether or not this theology of the sex fiends will carry the day and provide the platform for a Puritan Revolution of the 1970's remains to be seen. But one way or another, a sexual climax must come.

NOTE: Let it not be said—as some people certainly will try to say—that this book would put a damper on the fun of sex. Make the sex act as attractive as you can; attribute to it what you will of fun and thrill. Our thesis is simply that, in marriage (true marriage), sex is all that and more—much more.

But who can know this for a fact and testify to it as a fact except those who can speak from the experience of having been well married—and thus married for some

The Climax

time? But, by the very nature of the case, such people will all have to be over thirty and thus members of that generation who simply *can't* know how it is and whose testimony, therefore, automatically is discredited.

So what to do?

There is only one thing to do. If you are under thirty, determine to test for yourself sex by the marriage method, and then report back in, say, fifteen to twenty years. At that time you can try to convince your own kids of the truth of what we say. See you then!

Chapter Seven
(Or not a chapter at all,
depending upon how you count Afterwords)
AFTERWORD
by the Rev. Mr. Mather

Well, folks, that's the climax! And that's the book!

We asked Dr. Eller to stop at this point. (Actually, we unplugged his typewriter, tore the manuscript out of his hands, and rushed it to press.) Things were beginning to get out of hand; and besides, everyone knows that the only thing to do after THE CLIMAX is go to sleep—to attempt anything more would be *anti*climax.

There is not the slightest doubt in my mind that this book represents the stuff that revolutions are made of. The only question now is who will find it most revolting, the Puritans or the Impuritans. In the process of making that determination, we hope to sell copies to both.

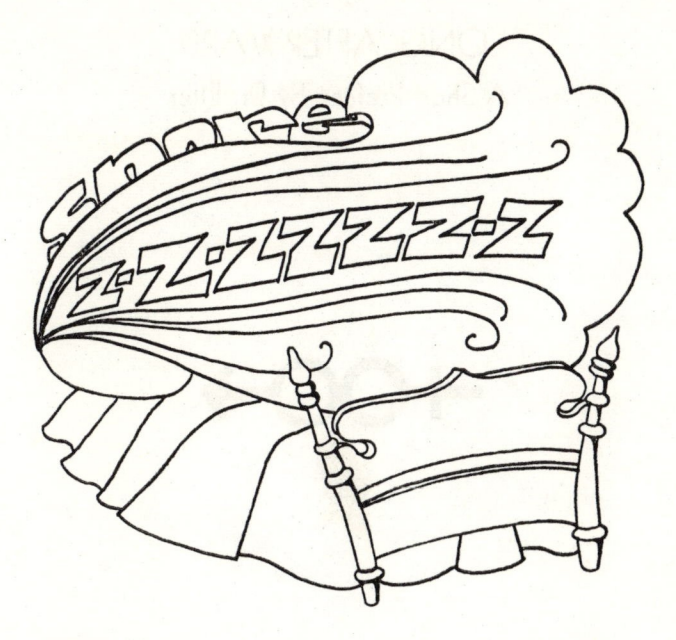

If you find that this book is influencing your sex life, you might consider giving it to a friend. After all, you shouldn't have to go Puritan all by yourself.

LONG AFTERWARD
A Short Preface by Dr. Eller

Other authors place at the beginning of their books a preface thanking various people for things of which the reader can have no comprehension at that point. For instance, how can the reader know that the typist did a good job until he sees how it looks?

I am rectifying that matter by putting the preface here—even though some of those about to be thanked would just as soon have had their praise before the book got read.

My thanks, first of all, to that distinguished pair, Cotton Picken Mather and Richard Armour, for their elegant and elevating contributions—without which this book would have been considerably shorter and perhaps some cheaper.

Prostrate Puritans Arise!
Be Free!
HIP HIP HOORAY
PURITANS are revoluted, too!
sex
PROTEST IMPURITANISM

The Sex Manual for Puritans

My thanks to Abingdon Press and Editor J. Richard Loller (fine Puritans all) for giving me a hard time from start to finish—for the good of the cause, naturally.

My thanks to Dr. Paul Popenoe and his American Institute of Family Relations, from whose newsletter "Family Life" (the best periodical in its field) anything in this book that sounds as though it might have a factual basis probably was taken.

My thanks to Dr. (M.D.) Reuben for having set up a prominent target that I could lean on or shoot at as the mood indicated.

Most of all (and here words fail me), my thanks to my wife Phyllis for . . . No, not for that! You know we Puritans don't discuss such things in public. For the inspiration of the book this little moron will thank her in private; what I wanted to thank her for here was typing manuscripts, reading proof, and censoring the first draft. (However, any misspelled words or other no-no's should be taken up with the publishers; they have had the manuscript since Phyllis did.)

So let's hear it for all these fine people and for all the poor, prostrate Puritans to whom the book is dedicated:

HIP, HIP, HOORAY!

(I know Puritans use "limb" in place of "leg," but what under the sun do they use for "hip"?)